TRUMPET
CHRISTMAS
DUETS

AF428944

TRUMPET CHRISTMAS DUETS

Eddie Lewis

Published 2023 by
Edward Lewis
A division of Tiger Music
Houston, Texas, 77089.

Cover art by Pearl Lewis

Printed in the United States of America

ISBN 979-8-89402-000-6

For information about individual or bulk orders of this title, visit
http://www.tigermusicstore.com

Dedicated to Ruth Lewis

I don't typically dedicate my work to people who have already died. Why I don't is a long story, but it can be simplified into saying that I want to honor people while I still have them in my life. There's nothing wrong, necessarily, with honoring people who have died. That's a good thing. However, there are so many people who need our love **now**, and so few opportunities to honor them, that it just doesn't make sense to me to invest into someone who can no longer appreciate that effort.

I've made an exception with this **Trumpet Christmas Duets** book because my mother was still alive when I began writing this page.

The original opening text was going to be:

> *"As we reach the final stages of putting this book together, my mother is lying in hospice. Naturally, I've been spending a lot of time thinking about her and the role she played in my life. If my father was the spiritual backbone of our family, then my mother was the meat on those bones."*

I was working on what came after that, trying to connect my mother to the content of this book, when we got the call that she had passed. Now, three weeks later, I've had lots of time to think about that connection.

Christmas was always a special time for my mother. Always!

When she died, she had four different Christmas trees that she put up every year, even into her 80's. She had Christmas decorations stored in almost every room of her house. At her church, my mother played a major role in preparing music and decorations for the Advent season. Every Christmas except her last, she made many dozens of Christmas cookies and other goodies to send to friends and family around the country. She was also proud to host Christmas parties for her "people group" and other groups she belonged to. Christmas truly was a very special time that my mother loved to celebrate every year.

Singing alto in church choirs for as long as I can remember, my mother probably knew all the words for the Christmas carols in this book. She used to fill the house with Christmas music and sing along as she went about her day. I think she would have been thrilled to know that I was dedicating a book of Christmas carols to her this way.

Contents

Introduction

Trumpet Christmas Duets is a collection of twenty-one of the most popular Christmas carols arranged for trumpet duet. The format for these duets is identical to the **Trumpet Hymn Duets** book we released three years ago, in 2020. In that sense, the **Trumpet Christmas Duets** book is a sequel to the **Trumpet Hymn Duets** book.

Both the **Trumpet Hymn Duets** book and this **Trumpet Christmas Duets** book are distinct from my other duets. As of today, we have released a total of five duet books, with a sixth (**40 Trumpet Player Duets**) intended for release shortly after this one. The other duet books, beginning with **Celebrations** (101 Original Trumpet Duets), are a mixture of educational and compositional duets. The **Trumpet Hymn Duets** and **Trumpet Christmas Duets** are not educational, and they are not my original compositions.

Everything I say about the **Trumpet Hymn Duets** is also true about this book. I have always said that the **Trumpet Hymn Duets** are "hymns first and trumpet duets second". The same is true with this new book. These are Christmas carols first, trumpet duets second. To achieve this objective, I honored the harmonies and moods of the original hymns/carols.

This is a very important distinction. People say that the duets in the other books are clever and compositionally interesting. And I appreciate their compliments. I am proud of those books, but the effort to remain true to the original hymns/carols makes these **Trumpet Hymn Duets** and **Trumpet Christmas Duets** stand out from the others. There is a beauty here that I could never accomplish through clever composition.

Progressive Order

I've arranged the duets in this book in progressive order. I put what I believe are the easiest duets at the beginning of the book and the most difficult ones at the end.

The overall skill level for the book ranges from intermediate to advanced. That said, there are no duets that go all the way to high C. There are only six B naturals above the staff and two B flats – in the entire book. Most of the duets in this **Trumpet Christmas Duets** book have G above the staff as their top notes.

The more advanced duets are only more difficult because of the sixteenth-notes, arpeggios, and intervals. Some of them also have interesting embellishments that can require some practice time, depending on the skill level of the trumpet player. All these things can be simplified by playing the duets at a slower tempo.

Meant for Performance

I have already played two gigs using the duets from this book. For both, we were hired to provide background music at social events at churches. In both cases, the audience was very pleased with the music. I have been doing trumpet duet gigs throughout my entire career. The most common type of Christmas duet gig has been at Country Club holiday parties where they like us to play Christmas carols as the patrons arrive. Sometimes we do these dressed in full Renaissance costume, performing on heralding trumpets. **Trumpet Christmas Duets** will work for any Christmas themed event.

Play-Along Recordings

While this book is not packaged with play-along tracks for you to practice with, these tracks will be released simultaneously, but separately from the book. The play-along tracks are available on iTunes, Apple Music, Amazon.com, Spotify, YouTube Music, and other music streaming services around the world. We will also be selling them as a download at our family music store, Tiger Music (https://TigerMusicStore.com). If you do not have someone to play these Trumpet Hymn Duets with, then we encourage you to use the play-along recordings.

Away in a Manger

"MUELLER" and "CRADLE SONG"

James R. Murray, William J. Kirkpatrick

arr. Eddie Lewis

34
40
rit.
C Faster ♩ = 96
45
mf
53
rit.
61

In the Bleak Midwinter

"CRANHAM"

Christina G. Rossetti, Gustav T. Holst

Arr. Eddie Lewis

Copyright © 2021 by Edward R. Lewis

C
25
D
Faster ♩ = 96
33
37
accel.

E
41
rit.
a tempo
45
rit.
"Amen" ♩ = 72
49
rit.

Quempas Carol
"QUEM PASTORES LAUDAVERE"

Traditional German
Arr. Eddie Lewis

C
D

Quempas Carol

Still, Still, Still

Austrian Folksong
Arr. Eddie Lewis

C
28
D
33
a tempo
rit.
37
41
rit.
E
Slower ♩ = 76
45
rit.

What Child Is This
"GREENSLEEVES"

William C. Dix, English Melody
Arr. Eddie Lewis

"Amen"

O Come, All Ye Faithful
"ADESTE FIDELES"

John F. Wade, Frederick Oakeley
Arr. Eddie Lewis

O Come, All Ye Faithful

45
f
51
E
56
rit.

It Came Upon a Midnight Clear

"CAROL"

Edmund H. Sears, Richard S. Willis
Arr. Eddie Lewis

Silent Night
"STILLE NACHT"

O Come, O Come, Emmanuel
"VENI EMMANUEL"

Traditional French
Arr. Eddie Lewis

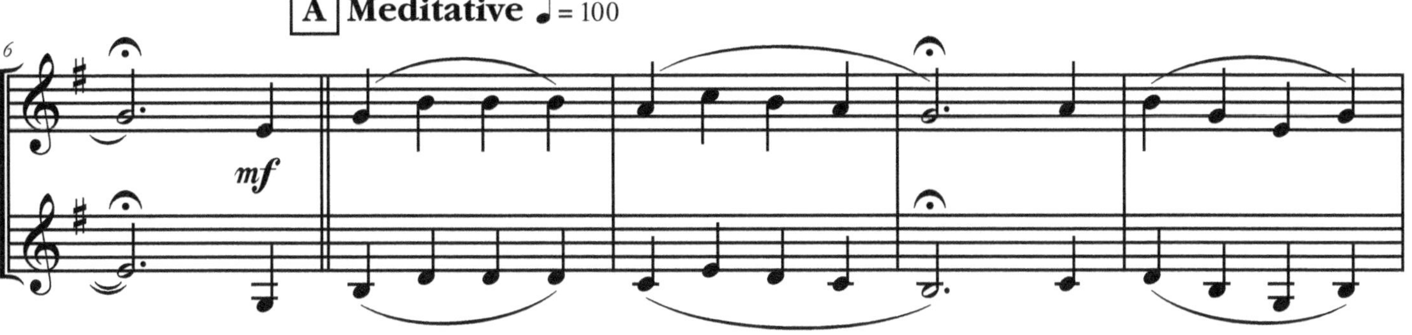

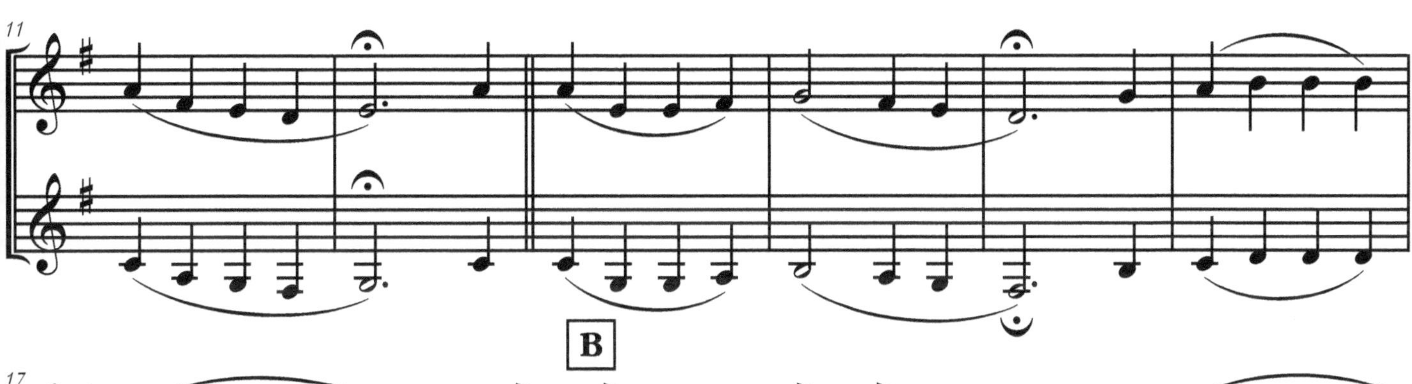

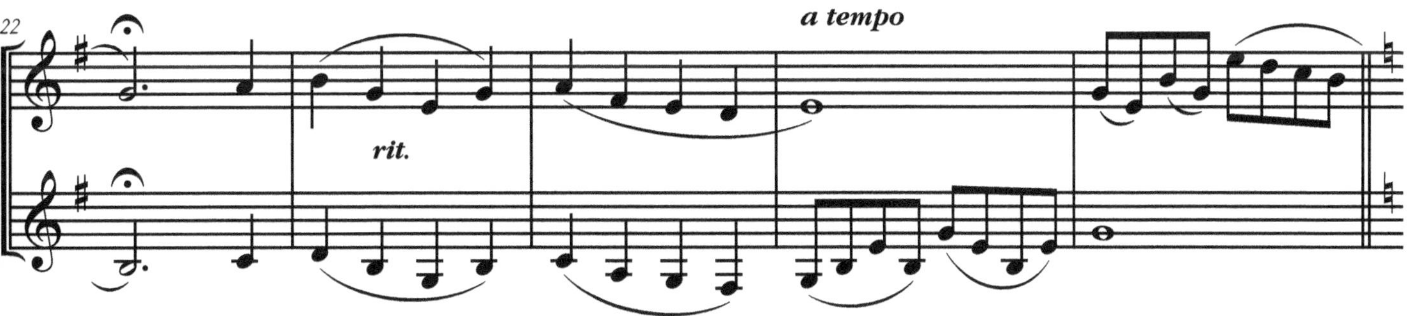

O Come, O Come, Emmanuel
C Faster ♩ = 120
rit.
mf
D
f
mf

O Come, O Come, Emmanuel

God Rest Ye Merry, Gentlemen

C
Lively ♩= 92
27
f
32
ff
D
36
mp
mf
41
46
f
mf

E
Optional "Amen"
rit.
rit.

O Little Town of Bethlehem

"ST. LOUIS"

Phillips Brooks, Lewis H. Redner
Arr. Eddie Lewis

rit.
rit.
C
a tempo

O Little Town of Bethlehem

The Holly and the Ivy

B
33
accel.
rit.
f
C
Faster ♩ = 120
41
49
D Tempo I ♩ = 112
53
rit.
mp
61
mf
accel.
rit.

The First Noel

The First Noel
B Faster ♩ = 100
accel.
Andante ♩ = 82
rit.
rit.
Faster ♩ = 100
rit.
"Amen" ♩ = 72

O Holy Night!
"CANTIQUE DE NOEL"

Placide Cappeau, John S. Dwight, Adolph Adam
Arr. Eddie Lewis

O Holy Night!

Deck the Halls
"NOS GALAN"

Deck the Halls

E
Faster ♩ = 100
F
f
mf
f
G
subito p
ff
H
mf

I
71
rit.
Slower ♩=92
f
ff

Hark! The Herald Angels Sing

"MENDELSSOHN"

Charles Wesley, George Whitefield,
Martin Madan, Felix Mendelssohn
Arr. Eddie Lewis

C
28
mf
32
D
36
f
ff
41
mp
ff
6/4
6/4
E
46
6/4
mp
4/4
f
rit.
6/4
4/4

Joy to the World
"ANTIOCH"
Isaac Watts, G. F. Handel
Arr. Eddie Lewis
Festive ♩ = 100
A
a tempo
f
rit.
mf
B
Copyright © 2021 by Edward R. Lewis
Trumpet Christmas Duets - pg 42

40
rit.
C   Maestoso
46
f
53
60
66

Angels We Have Heard on High
"GLORIA"

Angels We Have Heard on High
E
mp
f
mf rit.

Angels We Have Heard on High

Good King Wenceslas
"TEMPUS ADEST FLORIDUM"

John Mason Neale, John Stainer
Arr. Eddie Lewis

Trumpet Christmas Duets - pg 48

31
37
C Faster ♩ = 108
accel.
f
43
49
55

Good King Wenceslas

We Three Kings of Orient Are

"KINGS OF ORIENT"

John H. Hopkins, Jr.
Arr. Eddie Lewis

a tempo
B
a tempo
f
f
rit.

45
ff
49
mf
mp

Let All Mortal Flesh Keep Silence

"PICARDY"

Christina G. Rossetti, Gustav T. Holst
Arr. Eddie Lewis

Let All Mortal Flesh Keep Silence
31
37
43
accel.
B
Faster ♩ = 96
f
49
54

60
65
C Adagio ♩= 69
mf
rit.
71
76
rit.